MESSAGE FOR THE WEEK
Getting through the first year of grieving

*When you lose a loved one the hardest
thing is getting through the first year of pain.*

CHARLENE MABINS

authorHOUSE®

AuthorHouse™
1663 Liberty Drive
Bloomington, IN 47403
www.authorhouse.com
Phone: 1-800-839-8640

First published by AuthorHouse 5/4/2009

ISBN: 978-1-4389-5928-3 (sc)

Library of Congress Control Number: 2009903332

Printed in the United States of America
Bloomington, Indiana

This book is printed on acid-free paper.

Contents

Part II: Who Am I Without My Son?   41

Introduction

In the time of grief, we are angry, sad, and feel left alone. We have nowhere and no one to turn to. Death and heartache are uncertain. When tragedy strikes, our hearts are empty because there are pieces missing. You feel as though part of you has died with a loved one and can never return. But there is hope; there is a way to heal and see the light again. I have found inspiration through grief counseling, meditation, and reading positive books to help me cope with the death of my son, Christopher. First, I asked the question, "Why did this happen so suddenly?" This is so meaningless. But through prayer and hope, I realized my faith in God. I was so angry; I did not want to talk to anyone. Later, it occurred to me that just as I grieved there might be others grieving as well. I have seen a lot in my lifetime and still the question would remain, why? It took a long time for me to realize that we don't always have to answer questions just because someone asks; primarily because we are not always the holder of the answers. It is important for us to know that God is the keeper of all answers to all questions. And if we do not ask, we will never know. Throughout this process, I realized that God has been in the picture all of the time and has provided for me, continuously. My son committed suicide on September 16th 2007, and as you can imagine that was the beginning of a major change in my life.

Initially, I wanted to reach out for help for myself when I found myself reaching out to help other people. After Christopher's death I faced obstacles and challenges beyond belief. I would think about my son and how he must have felt when he had troubling thoughts on his mind, and couldn't explain what he was going through. On the day that he died I thought to myself, "What didn't I say that could have made a difference?" That was my starting point and I made a promise to myself that I would try to be open and truthful. For almost a year, I would send text messages via my cell phone, once a week to family members and friends with a little something to keep them going and to let them know that life isn't so bad. When I decided to compile the messages into a book, I provided bible passages as a guideline to each Message for the Week. Ironically, as I pursued this mission of helping others through God's word, I felt enormous healing myself. I received a lot of great reviews and compliments in return. But more importantly, reaching out to others in my worst time of trouble helped me to heal and understand that I did not grieve alone.

Thank you,
To all who helped make this book possible

In Memory of
Duane Christopher Peterson Jr.,
Loving son

Author: Charlene Mabins

My Beloved Christopher

Every day is a blessing from God
No reason to cry
So much to Live for
No reason to die
When I came into your life
There were no guarantees
Just love in my heart and a prayer
That when you needed me...
I would be there
For you...I only wanted peace
Love and tranquility...
No more drama, no more pain and instability
Our family was supposed to be your launching pad
So you could fly and we would watch you soar...
But you closed the door....
And as I watched the light dim
In your eyes, I searched for him
The boy who had so much to live for
And no reason to die.

Angela

Chris

Tears splash without taking shape
Landing, brushing the canvas of my face
I'm left mourning, lost in the days
If memory serves me correct, there are seven
But time seem to lapse, since my son was called to
heaven
I try to make sense out of gravity now
I sit on a chair; with four legs, and a back
And it seems to support me somehow
My thoughts are heavy, and my heart is under major
construction
The love for my son has been captured on film
And it's played back in my memory museum
I turn to Galatians 2:20,
"It is no longer I who live,
But it is Christ who lives in me
And the life I now live in the flesh
I live by faith in the son of God
Who loved me and gave himself for me"
And the tears that fall from my eyes, down to my
cheek
Are paintings of my son's smile
That I hold dear to me

By Tawanna Thompson

Part I

MESSAGE FOR THE WEEK

Message

Death has always held a big question mark

The tragic or unexpected death of a loved one always leaves questions for those left behind. One day we are laughing and talking, and the next they are taken away from this earth. Those who are left behind are left with grief beyond all comprehension. Who do I turn to? What's the next step? How do I cope? The biggest question of all, "Why am I here and they are gone?" How could God let this happen?

Message for the Week 1

I will remember the good and hold my head up high and know that someday it will be my turn to die. But in the meantime I will choose to do good here on earth until that day comes.

I will keep my mind focused on all that God has done for me in the past, present and future. He is my guide and my savior and he will show me the way.

Whenever your day seems rough or hard to deal with, ask God for guidance.

A short prayer to guide me in the right pathway

Open my heart Lord and make me steadfast. Give me guidance and strength.
Psalms 30:1-12; Matthew 6:9-13

Ask, believe and have patience.

Message

When it is time to really say goodbye to a loved one

When it is time to say goodbye to a loved one, the reality of death is solidified when viewing the remains of a loved one. To see my son silent and still with no signs of life, silenced me. You have so much to say but you're unable to say it, and you may feel it's too late; but it is not too late. When my son died, I wrote a very long letter and told him how much I will miss him and how I wished we had more time together. I know he is in a better place. I believe God sent me the messages to confirm that my son was with him. Just knowing that gave me the strength to take it day by day.

Message for the Week 2

We are not in control of everything that comes in our path. Instead we can allow ourselves to be guided by faith and realize that we only have control of ourselves and not others.

This is the time when dealing with unanswered questions come to consciousness but there are no answers. Try writing a letter to your loved one who has passed on. It may seem difficult but it will make you feel much better to tell your loved one how you feel.

A short prayer to guide me in the right pathway

I will keep my faith in the Lord and he will see me through.

Psalms 51:10-12

Ask, believe and have patience.

Message

After the wake

After the wake and funeral, people come to visit and the phone is ringing continuously. But the one phone call I was waiting for was from my son, just to hear his voice once more to convince me that I was in the middle of a nightmare. Then there are the constant reality checks from friends and family when they ask "Is everything ok?" To keep myself together and not let anyone see the horrific pain I was really going through I would simply say, "I'm fine!" I was not fine, but lost without answers. The questions that continued to resurface in my mind were "What could I have done? Why am I here?" I was angry with God and wanted to know why he didn't take me instead.

A year earlier, I survived a motorcycle accident that due to the extent of my injuries, doctors felt my survival was a miracle. But now I wanted to trade places with my son and I would ask, "God, why didn't you take me instead?" I would breakdown and cry and I could not get rid of the empty feeling. I still felt alone and believed no one could help. I went into automatic shutdown. A piece of me died with him. It felt like being in a jail with no bars but I still couldn't get out. Deep down inside you know that at any given moment you can walk to freedom because no one is holding you. The problem is you don't know how.

Message for the Week 3

When I have run out of answers and have lost my patience I will look to the Lord for strength and patience. God has been patiently waiting for me to return so he can heal my spirit and fill the emptiness. He will open doors, fill my heart and soothe my mind.

God has never left us, it is us who have left him, and he has been there all the time.

This is the time to ask God for the answers and to lead us in the right direction, continue to believe and have patience.

A short prayer to guide me in the right pathway

I will ask you all that I need to know and my meditation will fill my heart with the answers to keep me moving forward.

Isaiah 40:28-31; *John* 16:17-24

Ask, believe and have patience.

Message

The Impact

It was during this time that I tried to fight all of the negative things that were impacting my life. *The past*, what role did I play and what could I have done to alter these events. I would go to sleep at night, only sleeping a few hours at a time, knowing sleep deprivation would eventually take its toll. My thought process almost seemed like it was playing tricks on me.

The Blame Game, when someone dies or leaves suddenly, subconsciously we start an automatic analysis of what happened. Speculating and back tracking those very moments right up to the moment a loved one dies. You start to think about a certain age group, of what is acceptable and what is not acceptable. When a young person dies unsuspectingly or takes their own life, you want to know what happened and who is at fault. I had no answers, only a letter explaining why, and yet I still did not understand why or how this could happen. My son's life was just getting started and my life was beginning to slow down where I could finally take a breath of air and relax; get back into a routine, but No!

Message for the Week 4

When we have unanswered questions who do we turn to? How do we find comfort in dealing with the death of a child, parent, relative or friend? God has all the answers and we have to be patient and wait, believe and they will come in time.

God allows us to make choices and get all the questions out. Continue to take it day by day.

A short prayer to guide me in the right pathway

I will continue to ask all the questions I need to ask. I will wait and take the time out for the answers to come from God day by day.

Mark 9:14-30; Psalms 22:19

Ask, believe and have patience.

Message

Living day by day

Slowly living day by day and keeping my mind on the positive, I began to understand why certain events occurred. Sitting in solitude I opened my mind and heart. I could see that my soul had started to cry for help. Although I knew my mind, heart and soul needed help, they were functioning separately. My soul was fighting, and intertwined with my emotions, to keep me functioning. My heart was empty and my mind was confused. I found it very difficult and at the same time peaceful. As a parent, when you are fighting guilt and shame over the death of a child from the inside out, you start to wonder and think about taking the easy way out yourself. You cannot imagine living without your child. As I began to meditate, the words of support from family and friends took logical order and began to make sense to me. This is when I started to know that God was sending me messages through other people.

Message for the Week 5

When your soul cries for help that is its way of telling you that you need spiritual guidance and you need to seek help. Counseling helps, whether it is from an organization, from your minister or from a professional. It helps you to recover and know that you are not the only one in pain. However you are lead to seek help, seek it openly and honestly, it helps.

The best thing about God is that he knows just what we need in the time of trouble.

A short prayer to guide me in the right pathway

Heal my soul Lord and open my heart to seek and accept the help that I need.

2 Chronicles 20:9

Ask, believe and have patience

Dealing with self

Asking for help during the grieving period can be difficult. You know that you need some type of help, but from where and from whom? I thought to myself, "Well, if I ask for help from the church, people might think I'm weak and feeble, because I've never asked before. If I ask for help from my family and friends they are going to think I'm vulnerable and take advantage of me. If I ask for help from a professional counselor, they are going to say I'm mentally unstable." This is a challenge. How do I handle the task with all that has happened? I feel embarrassed and I don't know what to say. Nevertheless, I put on my coat of armor and asked for help anyway.

Message for the Week 6

Part of God's help is that he puts people in your life to help you. We just don't recognize this until later. When you are seeking help from others know that God is in the picture and working through them to give you the help that you need. He will give you signs to help you decipher what kind of help your soul needs.

Sometimes we don't have all the answers and may need a little help with hearing his soft voice talking to us. God speaks to us also through other people.

<u>A short prayer to guide me in the right pathway</u>

I will let you lead me in the right direction; seek help for my soul to go in the right pathway.
Ezekiel 36:26; Romans 8:5-9; 2 Timothy 4:16-18

Ask, believe and have patience

Message

The hardest thing to do

Boy was this hard to do! When I made the first appointment for counseling help, I decided I would try everyone. I went to a professional counselor. I went to my minister and I went to a Grief Supporters session for people who have lost a loved one. The second sign from God I received during this week was that everything is going to be ok. Each day I thought about my son and I remembered asking him, did he believe in God. I remembered one particular conversation we had about doing things for yourself, but always putting the Lord first in everything that you do. Then, I remembered I was starting to sound like a broken record that was constantly repeating the same thing. I wondered if he was really listening in those conversations. I am still bothered by the statement he made right before he died, "You think you know me but you don't!" At that moment, I knew I didn't really know the young man, my son had become or what he was thinking. I thought silently to myself only God knows our true heart and how we truly feel. We can only speculate on what others are truly thinking. I started to repeat in my mind, "We have a plan for ourselves and others have a plan for you, but God has the ultimate plan for you because he is the Master planner."

Message for the Week 7

When seeking help and thinking about the past it is good to keep an open mind and think outside of the box.

Sometimes we can set unexpected traps for ourselves. God can show us a way to get out.

The past can be tricky to handle if we don't know how; with God's help we can decode it. We can either learn from it or choose not to. Be careful to choose wisely and honestly.

The best way to learn from our experiences is to ask God to help us to see them for what they are.

A short prayer to guide me in the right pathway

I will lean toward you God for the help I need and accept all the help you are giving me, for you are my keeper and provider in all that I do.

Philippians 4:13

Ask, believe and have patience

Message

The choices made in the past

The choices I have made in the past were critical elements of today. When a loved one dies you are forced to think about what you have done in the past. I would ask myself did I do the right thing, or was I too hasty in my decision making. Did I do careless and thoughtless things to bring me to this point in my life? For weeks my self-esteem was on the back burner under a low flame waiting to boil at any minute. In my dreams I could see the light but could not reach it and it was impossible for me to grasp a grip on things. I knew my son's affairs needed to be completed. I did not want to go to the morgue and pick up papers about an autopsy, nor did I want to pick up his ashes from the funeral home, because of the pain deep down inside. This is the hard part, the last missing pieces; collecting the remains of your loved one. Burials are hard enough to handle but a cremation is something else! I received the phone call from the funeral home and they related that my ex-husband wanted to split my son's ashes between the two of us. In anger I asked the caller, "Did he write you a check? No!" I was determined not to split him up again. Frankly, I didn't want to share his ashes with anyone. I would keep him safe with me until I go. I was so distraught I even started to plan how I would go and where our ashes would be together. For a split second I really was thinking outside of the box, until then, I thought I was in control of my well being. Wrong!

Message for the Week 8

When we have tasks to do out of respect for a loved one, they are entrusting us to do the right thing. Although we have the choice to do wrong, I chose to do right. My will to live and do the right thing comes from God.

Sometimes we let anger take over and guide us to places we don't really want to go, but God is there to put us on the right track again.

A short prayer to guide me in the right pathway

When anger takes over God give me the strength to defuse it quickly and get back on the right track of my path to you.
1 Corinthians 14:40

Ask, believe and have patience

Message

Writing the thank you notes

I could not think about writing the Thank You notes. I decided to take a break and fly away somewhere, but nothing seems the same anymore. I still felt empty on the inside. A friend suggested that I come to Florida for a visit to get away. To my surprise my partner's co-worker offered us a voucher to stay at her Time Share location to express her condolences. The third sign that God is there. We went to Florida and during that whole time I was there it felt surreal and I felt like I was having an out of body and out of mind experience. Nothing was the same visibly or emotionally. I only wished my son was here with me. I kept thinking Chris would have liked this. I didn't feel any real enjoyment at all. I tried to make myself happy but deep down inside I was really sad. One night I was standing over the balcony in the room and thinking, "I should just jump right now what do I have to look forward to?" I thought to myself this pain is never going to go away and this sucks. No parent should ever experience the death of a child! Then I thought, what if I jump and survive and end up in a wheel chair that would suck! Or what if I have brain damage, which would suck too! Or better yet nothing happens, and I end up going to jail for trying to kill myself. Now that would really suck! So, I just sat on the balcony. I realized it was late and I needed sleep but it felt like someone else was there with me! I thought at that moment I was hallucinating. But a quick brush of truth flashed my way and I immediately felt and knew in my heart, Chris was alright! It was during this precious and enlightening moment I could hear my son's voice in my mind and heart saying, "Ma it's not time for you to go!"

Message for the Week 9

When we feel like life is not worth living, God always finds a way to let us know that it is.

Sometimes it seems like days get longer and slower and we cannot see beyond the next day but we have to live to see the next day.

A short prayer to guide me in the right pathway

I will live day by day and have the will to endure all that comes my way for God is with me.
2Corinthians 1:8-11

Ask, believe and have patience

Message

What to write

Getting to the Thank You cards was a huge task and took more strength than I thought. Half of the people who attended the funeral I didn't remember. I only remember asking God for help to get through the funeral. I didn't want to talk to anyone because I was just as distraught as they thought I was. It was my child who killed himself. I decided to write and mail a general statement to everyone who attended. At the time that was the only thing I could think to do. I thought about my parents' neighbor who lived next door and died from cancer. It was just a few months ago I went to visit him and he told me he was ready to leave this world. That is what I call a righteous death, when someone is suffering in this world and ready to die to free themselves from pain. Then I thought maybe he and Chris could hangout in heaven and occasionally check-up on us who are left down here. I used to think about life after death, now I never saw it the same way again.

Message for the Week 10

It is hard when a close family member or friend dies, but we have to remain steadfast and remember God is there with us all. Take time out, do a recap and remember them for the good. Say a prayer for the family or friends in pain.

Remember the person who has died and know that their family is in pain as well, say a prayer for them.

A short prayer to guide me in the right pathway

God keep them safe and strong and show them the same just pathway.
Zechariah 12:10

Ask, believe and have patience

21

Message

Life after death

Life after the death of a loved one can be surreal. Just watching my favorite crime shows on television was not the same anymore. It made me remember going to the medical examiners and the funeral home and seeing my son's body with the same autopsy stitches across his chest. He didn't look real to me at all. He looked like a shell or wax figure you would see in a museum. I thought to myself, "So this is really what it's like? Wow!"

I started to think, maybe I was talking too much and I should listen more. The emptiness in my heart was longing for my son to come back to me. I began to think I was watching too much T.V. at this point. I started to think maybe it was possible that he could come back to me in a different form. Soon I realized it was just my grief taking control of my imagination, and the T.V. shows I was watching were for entertainment only.

Message for the week 11

When you are grieving, the mind can play tricks on you and give you false hope. It is a way also for the mind to handle unbearable events. The brain is constantly kicking out information that we absorb everyday and processing many ideas. Grief is tricky.

Keep God on your side at times when in doubt.

A short prayer to guide me in the right pathway

Clear my mind, thoughts and keep me on the right pathway

to you. Open my mind, heart and soul, give me strength and guide me through this time in my life Lord.
    Ecclesiastes 6: 1-12

    Ask, believe and have patience

Message

Grief is tricky

Grief is tricky. One moment you think you are progressing and the next moment you realize you're not. Not long after my son's death my aunt passed away. Going to her funeral was the biggest test of my life. I thought I was strong enough to handle anything but it was an instant reminder. My heart went out to my aunt's daughter and my mother, because I knew they had many memories of my aunt. Deep down inside I really didn't feel any emotion and at the time I didn't know why. I felt relief in knowing she was in a better place. Shortly thereafter, my nephew and niece invited me to go bowling with them and I built up the courage to accept their invitation. All the way to the bowling alley I was telling myself everything will be fine. However, when I got there, I became consumed with memories of my son. I remembered going bowling with my son when he was younger, which gave me this incredible feeling that I had to get out of there. I could hardly breathe so I went outside of the building. Meanwhile, my nephew called to say he was running late but, still on his way. I waited until my niece and nephew arrived. I considered getting something to eat to pass the time so, I bought a tamale. But that wasn't it at all and I still wanted to go home. It was too much excitement. When my nephew and niece arrived I could see that this was their way of showing me how much they cared and were concerned. But I knew for myself it was not the right time for me to tackle an outing like this. It was too soon. As an aunt I wanted to be there for them, because I knew they were grieving too. I just couldn't do it.

Message for the Week 12

Sometimes it's difficult to spend time with people after losing a love one. The healing process has no time limit set for grieving. Keep meditating and don't give up.

God gives us the strength to deal with pain and let's us know when it is the right time to deal with people during this time.

A short prayer to guide me in the right pathway

This week I ask for strength, Lord. For I know now that I am weak and need your strength to get me through a tough time.

Psalms 94: 17-19; Proverbs 12: 25

Ask, believe and have patience

Message

Signs

I thought I was ready to take on some aspects of my life again, but, I quickly learned that I was not. I went back to work six weeks after my son died and jumped right back in, not clearly thinking things through. I just wanted to fill the hole in my heart and the loneliness I felt. Little did I know, my grief was strong and the devil was busy. I ended up quitting my job a few weeks later. This actually turned out to be a blessing in disguise. God sure does work in mysterious ways. Without the job I was now able to put all of my energy into school. I guess God thought I should do something a little bit more fulfilling! Initially I went back to school as a motivation technique for my son; it was just a way for my son to see me doing something positive. I know that I would not have made it this far without God. Honestly, there were some days I didn't know how I made it to class or was able to comprehend the material. I felt like I was not even there half the time. But, God was in the picture all the time. He sent quite a few people to look after me while I was at junior college and they know who they are. Thanks!

Message for the Week 13

When we feel like we are not worthy of anything good, and low in spirit, God is looking out for us. God will give us positive people and ideas to keep us moving forward.

A short prayer to guide me in the right pathway

I will keep on the right pathway you have set for me and not give up, for you are my savior.
Psalms 18: 25-29; Psalms 27: 2

Ask, believe and have patience

Message

Finding out

I would wonder why some people make it and some people don't make it? Like I said death does strange things to people! Painstakingly I started searching out ways of how I could be happy without my son here in my life. I kept thinking I would remember only the good things about him, although there were bad things too. How do I incorporate them into all that has happened? God knows everything and in time he will tell you the truth. One day I decided to go through my son's cell phone, I thought I had built up enough strength to do this. The phone didn't work initially because it had not been charged for months. I charged it and waited until my partner came home. We went through his phone together, text messages, photos and videos. There it was in black and white, except in color on his phone, my son's other-side. I guess the "in-thing" is to video your daily activities and his were very disturbing to see. I never thought you could live a double life, but he did. As always the parent is always the last to know. Now I knew what he meant when he said to me, "You think you know me, but you don't!" Then I thought, "Boy, the truth has finally come out." This was as much a disappointment as him killing himself. At one point, I wanted to pull him from heaven, beat him to a pulp and send him back. That is how angry I was! However, all was said and done and it was too late. So, now what are you going to do! I decided there is a reason why God wanted me to know this information now. I waited to get that answer from him too.

Message for the Week 14

When we are looking for answers, nothing seems like the right answers. We all have troubling questions and sometimes we get troubling answers. God knows what we can handle and what we can not.

Wait and have patience, and in time God will reveal all that we need to know.

A short prayer to guide me in the right pathway

I will wait on you Lord to give me the truth.
John 8:32; Psalms 145: 17-19

Ask, believe and have patience

Message

The Crying days

During the crying days I felt overwhelmed and could not stop crying. Those were the worst days of them all. I had no strength to pull myself together and felt I had no one to turn to. The mornings were the hardest to deal with. I didn't know how to shake myself out of it. I would just sit in disbelief, while losing all track of time. I would keep hearing a soft voice inside my head saying, "Everything is alright and you can make it." But everything isn't alright; I'm sitting here missing my son. As the tears flowed down my face, I just wanted to join him. I knew that I didn't want to die, but I wanted to see him again and ask him how he is doing. At this moment I realized I will never hold his hand again, nor will I be able to cut his hair or talk to him. We will never go shopping for clothes or play video games, but most of all I won't ever hear him say; "Ma!" and "I love you too!" I could go on and on but I think I should stop. Then I would stop crying and fall to my knees and ask God to help me! To give me the strength to pull myself back together, knowing that I have the memories of my son and I spent 18 years with him on earth.

<u>Message for the Week 15</u>

When we have days we think are unbearable, look to the Lord for help to make them bearable. There are those days when we just can't get it together to do simple things.

God is there to provide the help we need.

A short prayer to guide me in the right pathway.

Today is the day Lord where I need you the most to give me the strength.

Proverbs 3: 5-6; Exodus 15: 2

Ask, believe and have patience

Message

Struggling to see the outcome

I didn't want to look ahead. It was very hard to imagine a future without my son. I still take it day by day. I have been meditating now for weeks and I can feel the Lord moving me forward even though I don't want to move. I feel like a slow locomotive going "Beep, beep here I come on my way!" When I really want to be in a speed race and drive a Bugatti Veyron, the world's fastest car. Cars and material things, I think are the triggers and after my motorcycle accident, I decided to give my car to him or buy him a car. I think that's what hurts, I will never be able to buy him a car and go through those kinds of times with him. To see his face light up, and be surprised, these are the moments when you feel cheated. Feeling cheated took a lot out of me; it almost put a wedge in my relationship with God and also with people. I could feel myself slipping down a slope when feeling cheated. This has taken me months to figure out, dwelling on it too long would pull me back into "The Blame Game" and would give me trouble seeing the outcome.

Message for the Week 16

When we struggle to see the outcome and think about all the things we should have done with our loved ones, don't forget about all the things we have done. God has not forgotten.

A short prayer to guide me in the right pathway

I know that someday I will be with you Lord and my loved ones who are there. Until that time, I will stay close by your side for guidance and strength here on earth.
Philemon 1:1-25

Ask, believe and have patience

Message

Packing the clothes

Well it is time to pack his clothes and give away his things. During my early stages of grief over the loss of my son I found it strange to keep my son's material things. When family members died in the past I didn't think much about keeping their belongings. It was like a keepsake to remember a loved one. However, I found it very surprising that I really didn't keep many of my son's things. The only thing I kept was a shirt which had awards and ribbons attached that were from his school. I kept this shirt because I noticed he was proud of his awards. The rest of his belongings I donated to an organization that works with teenagers. At the time I was unaware of how much that helped me with my recovery and grief. I guess I didn't think much about it until now, writing the messages. It was hard enough walking down to the first floor of our home and seeing his room. Days after he died I would go into his room, and I could still smell the strong aroma of his Axe body wash and the subtle hint of his cologne. The room was still set up the same way he had it. Subconsciously, I felt if I kept his room the same way and all his things, maybe one day he will return. I received a phone call from my mother and she told me that I would have to eventually give him up and let go and turn him over to God. Deep down inside I didn't want to let go, I wanted to hold on for just a little while longer. In the end I thought maybe somebody needs this stuff and can use it more than me.

Message for the Week 17

When it is time to give your loved ones things away remember that there is always someone else who needs help, no matter how big or small. The gift of giving will ease that pain. It won't seem like it initially, but in time it will.

The gift of giving is the biggest gift of all.

A short prayer to guide me in the right pathway

This week I ask that you guide me Lord with the gift of giving and I will give whole heartedly.
Deuteronomy 15:7-11; Matthew 6:1

Ask, believe and have patience

Message

Day of having no thoughts

There are days of when you seemingly have no thoughts at all. I just sat there day after day like a blank canvas. I would let my mind wander off for a few hours and not think about anything. I thought to myself, these are the silent moments. I feel like I have too much time on my hands and too much of nothing to do. After awhile I would play a video game. Then, there it was my first kill shot. I aimed right for the head of my victim in the video game. Quick and easy is what I thought, quick and easy! I had a completely different approach to my game playing and I would remember my son saying, "You really are a game head!" Then I laughed out loud and said to myself, "Yeah, that's right!" It's funny how you think of such provable things and they turn out to be true.

Message for the Week 18

When your mind is blank, and it's a nothing to do day, don't give up, your mind is just processing all of what is going on around you.

God knows when we need a break and to just do nothing, he will give us rest.

A short prayer to guide me in the right pathway

This week I will turn everything over to you Lord.
Psalms 143:1; Lamentations 3:49-56

Ask, believe and have patience

Message

Dreading the holidays

Getting through the holidays can be difficult and create an overwhelming sense of dread. I tried not to think much about the holidays. Just marking the holidays on any calendar would make my heart begin to beat fast. Anxiety would sneak in and in one breath I would try to pull myself back to a safe place of thought. I would ask myself, "Should I stay at home or should I leave?" I wanted to do something to occupy my time and fill the empty space. The hours seem to pass by so slowly and the days were long and unbearable. For some uncanny reason I found myself getting through them with ease. In the mornings, I would pray and ask God for help, and then turn the day over to him. I wouldn't think beyond neither the next hour nor the minutes and I did not let the seconds bother me. I guess I made a conscious choice to Let go, and Let God. I lit a candle and said a prayer for Christopher.

Message for the Week 19

When it is time for the holidays to come, light a candle, say prayer and remember a loved one whom you have lost. When you are out among others, it is ok to bring up the memories of a loved one. They are still in our heart as well as in our mind, and that is ok.

A short prayer to guide me in the right pathway

I will continue to put all things in your hands Lord and

these days of passing through the holiday will help me know
that you are still by my side.
   Psalms 25:15-17

   Ask, believe and have patience

Message

I made it

I made it! I made it and that wasn't so bad. I got through it without a scratch on me. I thought to myself and said, "O Lord I made it through the holidays, I thought I wouldn't have the strength to make it but I did!"

Message for the week 20

When you make it through, remember God is in the picture watching our every move and he is continually guiding us through it all.

God is always there.

A short prayer to guide me in the right pathway

Thank you God, this week I will remember how far I have come with you by my side. Thank you God.
1 Peter 4:7-11

Ask, believe and have patience

Message

A quiet talk

I would quietly talk to my son on occasion, in my home, and initially I thought it was crazy. I would remember the conversations I had with him when he was alive, so what's wrong with now. I even asked the grief counselor if it was all right. "Just as long as you are not asking yourself questions and answering," she said. I laughed aloud and said, "Yeah, I know right!" I feel good, I was proud of my son and I respected him a lot. For some reason I knew he was with God and still looking out for me just as he did down here on earth. I realized now it was time to work on me and I had to be brave enough to do so.

Message for the Week 21

When God is working with us, we will begin to see the light. Stay close to him and keep making time to meditate with him daily. God will show us the way. If it makes you feel good to talk to your loved one who has passed on, it is alright.

A short prayer to guide me in the right pathway

I will continue to let you work your wonderful works through me, Lord
Numbers 6:22-27: Philippians 4:4-9

Ask, believe and have patience

Part II

Who am I without my son?

It has now been almost five months and one week and the hardest things I had to do was get through the shock of my son's death and the aftermath of what he was really up too. I guess nobody is really ready to deal with the death of a loved one, especially a child. I thought I had gone through everything in life, but nothing compared to this. When I thought about seeing him in the morgue, seeing him in a casket he didn't look the same anymore. I felt like this can't be real. You hope they come back to you, and somewhere between the 5th through 7th month I began to question who I was as a person without a child. I found it very difficult expressing who I was at times and started to punish myself for what my son did to himself. Yet I still wanted to make a go of it and find out who is Charlene, the person. I realized that I am still a mother and I am Christopher's mother. I remember when I applied for a loan at Northeastern University, I forgot to put single and instead marked parent with child/children. It was that simple mistake that gave me a reality check that I was now considered childless. I didn't really want to feel that way, however; that was the truth, and a constant reminder. There was no escaping that and these are the little things that make you question who you are as a person. I knew the New Year was approaching quickly and I began to really wonder who I was as a person, partner, family member and friend. Was I the person I was supposed to be in this world? Would I let my limitations get the best of me? Or would my confidence bailout and my ambition disappear? These are the things I went through with grieving at the same time.

Message

A new year

I'm in the midst of a new year! What should I do, how should I go on with all that has happened? I am in my last year of junior college and it is the spring semester. The one question I would eventually have to answer was, "Who are you doing this for?" Is it for me, or who? Dealing with yourself and finding out who you are as a person is quite hard to do when you haven't dealt with yourself for a long time. I never really put any focus on myself, except to survive and keep the bills paid as best as I could. Am I worthy of my own attention?

Message for the Week 22

When you start to evaluate your self worth and value take a look at your talents, your skills, and decide which ones work for you and which ones make you happy.

God will help you to decide

A short prayer to guide me in the right pathway

Lord you blessed me with the talent that I have and I will put it to use. Guide me with this talent as a tool for you Lord.

Ephesians 4:1-17

Ask, believe and have patience

Message

Who's on first?

Who's on first? Who will be the focus of my attention now? My son's death left me with a void in my heart because my entire adult life, up to now, had been devoted to his happiness and his well being. The decisions I made were based on Christopher's well-being and survival, so now, who will get my attention? Me? I don't think I really know how to do this. This is a question I will have to face, but I don't know how. My meditation and prayers will have to be my guide to defining this new person. How do I define myself? I asked God, "Who am I and what is my purpose?"

Message for the Week 23

God is who we should put first in our lives at all times and then everything else will fall into place.

A short prayer to guide me in the right pathway

I'm working my way toward you Lord and you will always be first in my thoughts, my mind and my soul.
Ephesians 1:11-12; *Revelations* 1:17-19

Ask, believe and have patience

Message

Family

When my son died I couldn't think about anyone else and it was not until several months later that I made a conscious effort to reconnect with my family. I wanted to build a relationship with them and re-establish some type of communication with them. However, now that I am in my forties, too many years have passed us by, but I still love them very much. I felt like it would be toxic for me to re-insert myself into their lives as well as them into mine. Being in solitude for so long has helped me a great deal to accept myself as I am and others as they appear to me. Nobody in this world is perfect and I have always accepted my family for who they are, they are my family.

Message for the Week 24

When we think about our family during the time of grief and pain, remember it is hard on the family as well, so keep an open door. When a loved one dies it is hard on everyone.

A short prayer to guide me in the right pathway

This week I will pray for family and friends. I will ask you Lord to give them relief and understanding.
Philippians 1:3-11

Ask, believe and have patience

Message

Partner for life

I didn't really think about how much my partner was suffering nor did I consider her feelings. I was so soaked with grief and I missed my son terribly. I did not pay attention to her pain. I would just go about my day and pretend like everything was ok with us and it was not. These are the conversations you really don't want to approach and, just wanting the days to slip by. This can cause a mountain of uneasy feelings that become a ticking time bomb ready to go off at any moment, and when you say the wrong word "Look out!"

Message for the Week 25

When your partner is suffering, don't forget they are suffering just as bad as you are.

Together all things can be worked out with God by your side.

A short prayer to guide me in the right pathway

This week I will pray for the both of us and ask you Lord to keep us on the right pathway.

2 Corinthians 1:3-7

Ask, believe and have patience

Message

Friends

You truly learn who your friends are during your time of grief. I have lost a lot of friends in my life. Sometimes I think about them and wonder how they were doing. I have come to realize that some people came in my life for a moment and some for a lifetime. Friendship was not one of my best qualities because my ability to trust was very low. The fact of the matter is that I didn't know how to be a friend. It wasn't until my late 30s that I decided to work hard at being a friend and putting a little bit more trust in people. I would hear sayings like "friends come and go, but God is always there" and throughout my life I have seen this happen. Finally, I figured out if I'm not a good friend then how could anyone else be a good friend to me, It was so simple!

Message for the Week 26

When friendship is questioned, think of God, he is the best friend in the world. Think of the good and remember he has never left you. Whether we have friends only for a moment, or for life time, work on being the best friend you can be. God can teach you something about being a friend, he has all the experience.

A short prayer to guide me in the right pathway

Help me Lord to be the best friend I can be.
Proverbs 16:28; 18:24; 19:4

Ask, believe and have patience

Message

The Accident

I often mention my motorcycle accident and for awhile I let it get me down. I think about my son quite often and sometimes this gets me down. I have often let doubt enter my thoughts. I would think if I had been closer to God maybe none of this would have happened. Then I would laugh silently and think to myself, "God gave us the free will of choice. God did not tell me to hop on my bike and ride off into the sunset, nor did he tell my son to take his own life." I was not putting God first and taking the time to think things over and make wise decisions. At that moment it came to me that there are good accidents, and there are bad accidents and I should learn from them all. The consequences will impact us either way; we utilize them good or bad. I choose the good and decided whatever comes my way I know that God is by side. I only wish Christopher would have known that too.

Message for the Week 27

When we have accidents, although they are hard to explain, know that God is by our side.

God knows everything.

A short prayer to guide me in the right pathway

You have never left me Lord and you have always been here, so I thank you.

James 1:2-7

Ask, believe and have patience

Message

A slip of the tongue

I would often say things like, "So What; I don't care, and whatever." I didn't know how big of an influence these phrases would have on my daily living. Whenever I got sad and started thinking about all the pain that I've been in, I would say those words. My behavior began to reflect this particular thought process and what was on the inside, sure came out on the outside.

Message for the Week 28

When we think negative, we get negativity in our lives. If we think positive and know that God is good, it will show in our walk, talk, and what we do.

God is good.

A short prayer to guide me in the right pathway

I will stay positive and release all negative thoughts out of my mind, body, and soul. I will let you work your wonderful, positive energy through me Lord.
Psalms 35:38; 39:1-13

Ask, believe and have patience

Message

Do you know yourself?

Who am I? What kind of person do I truly want to be for the rest of my life? It's funny to ask that question when you are in your forties, some people begin planning their lives when they are in their 20's others in their 30's. Not me! I think I walked around lost for years not knowing who I was and had no direction. I guess I could say I'm a late bloomer! For a long time I just accepted myself as a mother and that was that. Then, in the blink of an eye the years flashed before me. It seemed like, just yesterday my son was a baby, an adolescent, a young man in college and then, we were having his funeral. Now, it's come to the point in time when I have to deal with myself. What do I do and where do I go? I will always be a mother as long as I live. I'm his mother and I love him very much.

Message for the Week 29

When the loss of a loved one becomes a loss of self, take time out to meditate with God. Focus on the good in you and ask God to help you find your way back to him and who you are meant to be.

God knows who we are truly meant to be, ask him

A short prayer to guide me in the right pathway

I will focus on what I am truly meant to be and let you lead me in the right pathway, for you are my leader.
Galatians 5:15-18

Ask, believe and have patience

Message

Confidence

Confidence! Boy, did I fall short when it came to being self-assured and having self-confidence. I second guessed myself as a parent, person, and professional. That little bit of doubt surfaced and changed my whole outlook on life and making wise choices. I think about the "if I, coulda, woulda, shoulda" and then I think about I should have asked God first.

Message for the Week 30

When your confidence is low, ask God to give you assurance again and believe that with him all things are possible. There will always be obstacles in our lives however with God by your side they will not be obstacles at all, just life.

When God is by your side, nothing can stop you, believe.

A short prayer to guide me in the right pathway

I will have confidence and know that you are by my side guiding me in the right direction and leading me to my goals. With you anything can be done, this I pray.

1 John 5:14

Ask, believe and have patience

Message

Ambition

Ambition! There is good ambition and there is bad ambition. I knew when my heart was not in the right place the grief was distorting my sense of right and wrong. My mother would tell me "a slow go is a honest and for sure go." A fast go is almost always certainly a quick death sentence. Living the fast life doesn't pay at all. Throughout my life, I have come face to face with uncertainty. Karma will sneak up on you and capture your whole being before you know. So, the quote an eye for an eye doesn't always apply. Sometimes it is best to just let God handle things. I have learned that the hard way.

Message for the Week 31

When ambition gets out of hand, just remember God can tone it down for you and put you back on the right path to your goals. Have faith in him and believe.

God wants you to succeed, have faith and believe.

A short prayer to guide me in the right pathway

I will keep my faith in you Lord and be ambitious with you in prayer and meditation. My success starts with you, for you are my light.

Matthew 25:13-21;

Mark 12:1-12; Luke 12:13-21; 15:1-10

Ask, believe and have patience

Message

Seeing some light

Am I beginning to see some light? I'm beginning to think about, "What do I want to do and how do I make myself happy?" As a parent, when your child gets to the age where he /she can almost stand on their own, you think that you are beginning to see some light at the end of the tunnel. That's how I was feeling before Christopher's suicide. Yes, parents can be fooled by their children! I truly thought that I knew my child, but instead he knew me better. We think they are not watching, when in reality they are.

It's hard to think about this is the time that children go off to college because I was so proud of him. I did not think I would be starting a new life without him. At every waking moment you don't know if you should feel sad or make yourself happy. The thought of happiness makes you feel guilty. I had to figure out how to not feel so guilty and just work on happiness and free myself from being guilt-ridden.

Message for the Week 32

When seeing the light for happiness is hard to do this is the time we need God to surround us and we keep meditating and praying the most. It is hard to break depression, grieving and sadness. Keep in mind with God all things are possible. Turn it over to God.

God, and our loved ones whom we have lost, do not want us to be sad but instead to find peace and happiness.

A short prayer to guide me in the right pathway

You are lifting me from all that pains me Lord and I will keep my focus in the light that you are leading me to, peace and happiness!

Isaiah 32:1-20; 2 Timothy 6:3-6

Ask, believe and have patience

Message

What is the truth?

What is the truth? The truth for me is that I will have to turn everything over to God. I realized in the last few months that I can not fight this kind of grief alone. As the months passed, I finally accepted that continuously asking the question of "Why?" wasn't helping, but prolonging the grieving. So, I chose to give him up to the Lord and live. Chris is with the Lord now and he is all right! Sounds strange but once I acted in my faith things began to slowly get better for me. It's going to be all right. My mother would tell me in one of her famous quotes, "Life is uncertain but death is for sure!" You know, she was right. I don't always want to hear the truth but it sure does help.

Message for the Week 33

When the truth reveals itself we don't always want to hear the truth and at times it hurts. The truth of the matter is that the truth really does help heal and it helps us to live. When you are ready let go and turn it over to God.

God is truth.

A short prayer to guide me in the right pathway

I will turn my life over to you Lord because you are the truth and the light. I release my loved one over to you because I know you are our keeper. Amen

Matthew 16:24-28: John 1:14

Ask, believe and have patience

Message

When doors are opening

Doors are opening! At first I didn't see anything unusual happening at all. I just went about my day doing what I thought was best for me. The closer I got to God the more I started to see.

This is hard to explain. In my best words, you just know and it feels good. I told myself I must remain humble, not be a hypocrite, nor should I be judgmental and keep in mind "let go and let God." You know the old saying elders would say, "You tried everything else so why not try God," seems hard to believe but it is true.

Message for the Week 34

When doors open keep in mind they are opening because you are getting close to God and he is showing you that he has never left.

A quote: "When one door closes another one opens." Keep this in mind as well.

A short prayer to guide me in the right pathway

You are my guide Lord and you are the key to the doors.
1 Peter 1:3-9

Ask, believe and have patience

Message

The birth date

Today is Christopher's birthday. My son was born May 31, 1989, exactly 19 years ago and it was his plan to never make it to this age. I had been dreading this day for eight months and now it was here. I didn't want to look back to the past but I couldn't help myself. I tried to remember the happy moments, but I could only focus on the fact that he was no longer here. I found myself slipping into depression. I thought I was strong and could handle this, but I couldn't. I give all the credit to the Lord for helping with getting me through my son's birthday.

Message for the Week 35

When a loved one's birthday comes light a candle, meditate, and thank God for the moments that you have had with him/her. Take the day and do something you would have liked to do with them but didn't get a chance. Share the day with family members or a friend, it helps.

A short prayer to guide me in the right pathway

I will celebrate the moment for I know that my loved one is with you Lord.
Philemon 1:1-25

Ask, believe and have patience

Message

Starting over, new goals

Now I have to begin starting over and creating new goals! To complete who I am I have to realize and accept that I will enter a new life without my son. I know he will always be in my mind, heart and soul. I could get factual about it, or even statistical about it, however, I would rather be real. Starting over is not easy at all and I was scared to go back into the world and do it again. I really felt alone and I backed away from opportunities when faced with them. As I meditated and prayed for strength and guidance I felt like something came over me and said, "What are you thinking, you are not alone in this world you have me!" I realized I wasn't alone my grief just made me feel that way. Believe it or not things got easier with starting over.

Message for the Week 36

When starting over becomes scary we tend to forget about God and we think he has left us, but he hasn't. Put him first in everything that you do and see what he can do. With God by your side there is nothing you can't do. Look at the talents you have, go back, filter through the skills that you have learned and put them to work.

Ask God for guidance, you will see them come to life, stay positive and believe

A short prayer to guide me in the right pathway

I will not let doubt enter my relationship with you Lord but instead believe, I'm never alone with you in my life.
Isaiah 30:15-21: Hebrews 3:14

Ask, believe and have patience

Message

Being practical

I never really knew what I could do because I didn't really try hard at much of anything. I guess you might say I was going along with the flow of things. I didn't put my best foot forward and kick down some doors. When opportunity knocks I should have been prepared, nevertheless I was not. I think I had "being prepared" and "hard work" confused somewhere down the line in my growing up. "Now what would God do in this case," I thought. Well, he would have been prepared and worked hard to achieve his goal. I can not be lazy about doing and believing. I must be practical.

Message for the Week 37

Being practical only means realizing your true strengths, weaknesses, and knowing what you are truly capable of doing. However to recap from weeks 31-36, know that God will help you discover all strengths and weaknesses. Ask him for help and he will uncover the true you and the person you should be.

With God's help, you can mold yourself into the person you are meant to be.

A short prayer to guide me in the right pathway

Mold me Lord into the person I am meant to be.
Galatians 4:8-11

Ask, believe and have patience

Message

New life, second chance

Wow! This is all that I could say as I reached this point in my life! A few weeks ago I completed my A.A. and this month I started my first class for my B.A. at Northeastern IL University. To be honest I didn't think I would get this far. I did, and in some crazy sort of way I feel relieved. It is like a breath of fresh air being born again and given a second chance. Although I knew my son was gone, I felt as though my son had never left me but was just in a new form of energy. I would jokingly think that Christopher was in heaven saying to God, "Help my Momma!" My faith tells me that God has a sense of humor too, and then I would laugh out loud. To really know that God is by your side really does feel good. I like to think I have an extra angel by my side too, Christopher.

Message for the Week 38

When feeling like we are being reborn and given a second chance, don't forget about God, keep meditating and praying.

Stay close to God and keep in touch with him regularly.

A short prayer to guide me in the right pathway

I can see the light and you are helping me heal, I will keep in touch with you Lord.
Psalms 71:23

Ask, believe and have patience

Message

Obstacles

Managing my thought process to work between my grief and my studies was initially overwhelming. But, I couldn't let these obstacles deter me. Don't be afraid of obstacles. I call it maintaining awareness, and understanding that God didn't promise me that life without my son was going to be easy. I knew my journey without my son in my life would have its obstacles but I should not be afraid of them. Disappointment and anger are serious obstacles to your healing. Trust in God to protect and guide you.

Message for the Week 39

When obstacles arrive, don't be afraid to tackle them. Think of God as your offensive line protecting you, knocking them out of your way to keep you moving forward.

God will guide you safely through your obstacles.

A short prayer to guide me in the right pathway

Whenever obstacles come my way this too I will turn over to you Lord to guide me in the way I should go.
Psalms 62:5-8

Ask, believe and have patience

Message

Stepping away to remember

I have experienced many things in my life good and bad, but hindsight is the worse. During this time I began to relive and re-evaluate the days and events that led to my son's tragic decision. I kept thinking if I only knew then what I know now, maybe the outcome could have been different! Maybe I could have said something else to Christopher that might have altered his decision. Three days before Christopher committed suicide we had a very long and intensive conversation about his life and his future. I thought since he was eighteen years old and appeared to be doing relatively well in school, he was ready to fly and soar on his own. I told him that I would support him in his decisions and would always be there for him. But today I realized that you can never really know what a person is thinking or deciding. You can only hope they are thinking about what's best for them, as you are.

Message for the Week 40

When you step away to remember keep in mind that no matter how hard it seems it is your way of getting a clear understanding of what happened. That's okay. Just remember God already knows before you do. It is okay to remember when you're grieving; it helps you to figure out your path to healing.

<u>A short prayer to guide me in the right pathway</u>

I listen to your soft voice Lord, for me to do what is right on my pathway to heaven.
1 Timothy 6:3-10

Ask, believe and have patience

Message

Hit a brick wall

I have hit several brick walls on my journey to the right pathway. I have always said, "The devil is busy." In the past I would say that and make light of it. I knew that it would be a struggle to be what God wanted me to be but I was determined this time the brick wall is coming down! I have thought about my son's death and I know a lot of people will not agree with me, however; I feel God permitted all of this to happen for a reason. I have made up my mind, and I'm sticking with God.

Message for the Week 41

When you hit a brick wall don't give up, hang there and keep believing.

God is there to help you break through the brick wall.

A short prayer to guide me in the right pathway

I will not let anything disturb my relationship with God. Joshua 6:1-27

Ask, believe and have patience

Message

Hope they come back

There were many days I would wake up in the morning and wish this was all a dream. I would be hoping he could come back! I would go downstairs and there was my constant reminder, his ashes sitting in his room, which we have now converted into an office. The pain of reality hits rapidly as I come back to my senses. I miss him more than ever.

Message for the Week 42

When we are hoping they come back, they have never left, not from our hearts. There will always be a time, a situation and a moment that we wish our loved ones were still here with us. This is the time to take a moment before continuing our everyday lives and think about something good you have enjoyed with your loved one. It helps.

Sometimes we cry, we feel sad, and sometimes we smile. Just remember God is there with us.

A short prayer to guide me in the right pathway

I know you are keeping them safe until it is my time to leave this earth Lord and until that comes I will put all my trust in thee to lead me.

Proverbs 15:13; Malachi 3:16; Philippians 1:3-7

Ask, believe and have patience

Message

Dreams

What are dreams made of? There are many people who talk about their dreams, for some people dreams are far larger than others, and some people believe in them and some don't. I think we give up on our dreams far too early in life. I realized that dreams don't end until you die and leave this earth. I wished I could have told my son these few little words during the times when he was down, "You should stop concentrating on dying and start living!" Why didn't I have the right words to say to him until now! I always felt I was two or three steps behind him, right on his heels and speeding up fast. However, he was eighteen years old and I couldn't keep up. I thought he could take off on his own and fly with all that I had already taught him. As a parent you pray everyday of your life, for your children. Today I feel cheated a little bit in life. I would have liked to see him become a full-grown, educated, young black man. Nevertheless, I am thankful for the glimpse of how it would have been. Even though it is difficult, I think I can live with that.

Message for the Week 43

When we give up on our dreams we lose out on God's wonderful work with us. It is hard to keep dreaming when we lose a loved one but we should not give up. Grieving and dreaming are not easy, keep meditating, stay close to God he will open doors and just think you have an extra angel in heaven on your side helping those doors open.

Remember God does not want you to give up, nor does your loved one who has passed away.

A short prayer to guide me in the right pathway

I will keep meditating Lord and I will not give up on my dreams, for you are my guide.

2 Chronicles 5:13; Acts 2:17; 2 Corinthians 12:7-10

Ask, believe and have patience

Message

Regaining your focus

I talk about meditation so much because without it, I would not have gotten this far. I make time in the morning, no-matter if it is five or twenty minutes and I talk to God about everything. I use this time to center myself and separate myself from the drama of the world. Reading the bible helps me to stay focused and it is also my tool for everyday life situations. I believe that having a healthy spiritual being is worth more than anything in this world. I believe every individual's religion is his/her own. I don't think you should force religion or any other ideologies on others. I also believe there is a right way and there is a wrong way to express your beliefs. I don't believe in judging people. I have learned over time not to focus on the world for what it has to offer me but instead focus on what God has to offer me. Initially, I thought it was very hard to do and now I can not live without taking time with God each day. Even when I am at a low point on a difficult day he makes the day seem better.

Message for the Week 44

I DEFOCUS the world and center myself with meditation in the mornings or, whatever time is good because God is always there, waiting. We can meditate with God and energize our spirit again. I call it filling your spiritual tank, except you don't have to pay, it's free. Talk to him.

Stay focused on God and he will help you handle any situation that comes your way.

A short prayer to guide me in the right pathway

Each and everyday Lord I will take this time out and meditate with you.

Psalms 5:1-3; 42:8

Ask, believe and have patience

Message

Negative energy

It is very easy to let negative energy into your life and damage all of the good energy you have achieved. Whenever I think about all the negative things that have happened to me, I realize that I have the choice to think of them as an experience to learn from or not. This has been a tumultuous year for me and yet I remain dormant. As I approached the 1 year anniversary of Christopher's death I could feel the anxiety merging with my grief. I guess I'm waiting until that day I can once again see Christopher, except it will not be in this life. A friend told me that I was punishing myself and forcing myself to go through unnecessary pain. At the time I didn't think about it that way, however later I did; and to be quite honest, for months, that is exactly what I was doing. The mind is strong and it has a way of dealing with trauma. I think if anybody understood me it would be God.

Message for the Week 45

When you start to feel negative energy coming, it's ok, that is what makes us human. But recognize that you are equipped with positive energy from God that will re-energize you and help you pick yourself up and keep moving forward.

A short prayer to guide me in the right pathway

Lord today I'm at my weakest and I need you to give me the strength so I can keep moving forward, Amen.
Psalms 42:1-11

Ask, believe and have patience

Message

Strength

When I think about being strong, what does that mean? What does it mean to anyone? Where does our strength come from? I know it comes from God! When I'm at my weakest and don't feel like going forward that is when God steps in and says, "It is alright maybe you need a break to replenish your strength." How do I know this? He shows me everyday! I could say "Sure I did it all by myself and I didn't need any help at all!" This would be taking all the credit, which I do not deserve. The credit goes to God for giving me the strength.

Message for the Week 46

Your strength comes from God. God only asks that you believe. My choice is to believe.

A short prayer to guide me in the right pathway

I choose to give my soul over to you Lord 100 percent and more. I turn all my situations over to you, for you are my provider and keeper. I know you will lead me in the right pathway Amen.
John 3:1-36

Ask, believe and have patience

Message

Overcoming

Losing a loved one is not easy and life can never just go on as usual. Even with all that is said and done, you still find yourself thinking about what could have been. A few weeks before my son's date of passing, I began having nightmares and feeling anxious. I subconsciously wanted the month to be over and I told myself, "This too will pass!" However, quite the opposite happened and time started to slow down, almost standing still, everyday seemed longer than the next. I decided to take it day-by-day. I could not find any rationale for the irrational act.

Message for the Week 47

When a moment of tears set in, we try to find comfort in the past. What is done is done and we as humans can not change what has happened. However, we can change the present and hope for the best in the future. It is ok to cry, it's ok to feel, it is ok to let go. It's ok to remember, and it is ok to know God is there with us through it all.

A short prayer to guide me in the right pathway

Thank you Lord for being there with me through it all. I give thanks to you this day.
Colossians 3:17

Ask, believe and have patience

Message

Recovery

The way you handle grief can make you strong or weak. Some of us recover quickly, and jump right back on track to succeed over our misfortune. While some of us do not recover so quickly and stagger along dwelling on the past. What I have noticed with myself, is I have always been caught in the middle. Sometimes I have the strength to go on and other times I just stagger along. I have been working very hard to correct this but as you can imagine it is very difficult to do. There are lonely days when I wish the time would fly by, and there are days when I just want to slow down and take it easy. I could go down a list of things that I should not do again in this lifetime and I would probably have an excuse for every one of them. However, I have to admit if God were not there to help me, I would not be here right now writing these messages. I believe everyone has a story to tell and each story is unique in its own way.

I wrote this book to let people know that there are going to be difficult moments of why, how, and what could have been. However, I have come to learn that without God's help I would have not made it. He sent people into my life who understood and helped me. He has opened doors that seemed impossible, and best of all, he has given me a chance to find him again.

Message for the Week 48

When grief comes our way, it is hard to recover and

get back on track. However, we have to remember that this too shall pass because God is always in the picture. Remember, do not just pray and meditate when things are going bad, stay in touch with him through the good and bad times.

A short prayer to guide me in the right pathway

I will always keep you close to my spirit. Lord, you are my provider and with you, all is possible.
Psalms 70:4; Philippians 4:4-8

Ask, believe and have patience

Message

Your story?

Writing a story! Everyone has a story to tell that is why I have decided to tell mine.

Don't keep your story bottled up let it out and maybe you can help someone as well.

Message for the Week 49

When it is time to write your own story, tell God first. Go back and remember how you felt and look at how far you have come with healing. The pain of losing a loved one never goes away. However; now, you are equipped to handle the pain of grieving a little better.

_____

_____

_____

_____

_____

_____

_____

_____

_____

_____

_____

_____

_____

_____

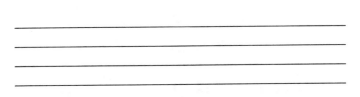

A short pray to guide me in the right pathway

God I know now you have been guiding me and there is a time for everything. This is my story!
John 12:1-25; John 14:1-6

Ask, believe and have patience

Message

When it is time to tell people your story

When is it time to tell people your story? The hardest thing I ever did was to learn how to open up and dismiss my silence. I wanted to take time and let God give me all the facts first and then make sure it was properly disseminated. I decided not to do the blame game, or have hatred in my heart. The information you receive after a loved one passes away can be devastating and this is when you put the missing pieces into place, no matter how long it takes. I was angry and overwhelmed with the information that I received about my son. But as hard as it was to know, I went to God to clear it up and reconcile my feelings. In time, he removed the cloud. I have a better outlook on life now and I am not blind anymore.

Message for the Week 50

When it is time to tell people your story make sure you get all of your facts in order. Make sure you have more then one side of the story. Most importantly, make sure you are comfortable and clear headed when telling your story. Here are a few more lines to practice writing your story.

Sometimes practice makes perfect.

_____

_____

_____

_____

_____

_____
_____
_____
_____
_____
_____
_____
_____
_____
_____
_____
_____
_____
_____

A short pray to guide me in the right pathway.

I have learned something new this week Lord and I thank you.

John 14:12-14

Ask, believe and have patience

Message

Ask, believe and have patience

What I have realized since my son's death is everything takes time and no-matter how long that may be, people heal in different ways. I have found out there is no quick solution and there is no ceiling on pain and disappointment from people. I realize that the only person we have control over is ourselves. It is up to us to learn how to have compassion, understanding and the courage to do what is right. Through all of the grieving and pain, the truth of my situation is that I have learned to keep God right by my side.

Message for the Week 51

When it is time to move forward in our lives it is not an easy road but if we ask God for help, believe and have patience he will walk us through anything.

A short pray to guide me in the right pathway.

I thank you Lord because this week I have found out that I am a living witness that you are truly real. I thank you for walking with me through this time of pain and making me stronger, Amen.
Matthew 7:7-12

Ask, believe and have patience

Message

Your prayer

We can read all of the prayers in books to help us say what we can't get out. However the best prayer of all is the original prayer that comes from our hearts. The prayers that I gave to you are prayers that came from my heart and now you can write prayers from your heart. Talk to God and let him know how you really feel and pray in your own words.

Message for the Week 52

When it is time to pray, it helps to pray in your own words. Say what ever comes to you because God knows your heart, mind and soul.

A short pray to guide me in the right pathway.

_____

_____

_____

_____

_____

_____

_____

_____

Colossians 3:12-17

Ask, believe and have patience

Charlene Mabins is a former Barber stylist and after having dead-end jobs for years, decided to go back to school in her late 30's, as a single parent. She thought she'd gone through everything good and bad in her life until September 16, 2007, when her son Christopher committed suicide at the age of 18, and left a note saying, "I love you mom and wish you to happiness." This was the beginning of her life without her son. The loss of a child is not easy and going through the stages of grief was a road she was not expecting to travel. She is a currently a student in the social work program at Northeastern Illinois University in Chicago. Charlene decided to write about her grieving process to tell how she was able to deal with her grieving and the ups and downs of the grieving process that she experienced. She is hoping she can help someone else by sharing her story.